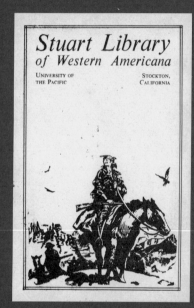

MILLER, Alfred J.   Braves and buffalo; plains Indian life in 1837.
University of Toronto, 1973. 176p (Public archives of Canada)
73-85088. 15.00.   ISBN 0-8020-2093-3

Traveling across the Great Plains and the Rocky Mountains in 1837
Baltimore artist Alfred J. Miller recorded his view of the country and
its inhabitants in watercolor. Commissioned by Captain Steward,
Miller accompanied a rendezvous caravan en route to Green River,
Oregon. In *Braves and buffalo* 41 Miller watercolors offer a brilliant
look at the West during a period when the white man was still only an
occasional visitor. Miller's work is important not only for its value
as fine art, but also as a historical and ethnological record, though the
ethnologist should be wary of relying too heavily on the Indian para-
phernalia. In addition, Miller, like James F. Wilkins (*An artist on the
Overland Trail*, 1968), who traveled much the same route a decade later,
kept notes on what he saw. These notes and comments published with
the watercolors offer a vivid view of the attitude of the artist toward
his subject. *Braves and buffalo* is well illustrated, though no effort
seems to have been made to place the watercolors in a chronological
sequence. It can serve as a reference for students of history and art
at any level and is an enjoyable book for recreational reading.

Braves and Buffalo

Plains Indian life in 1837

Alfred J. Miller was born in Baltimore in 1810. He studied in the United States, France and Italy. After returning to North America he made his reputation with the brilliant water-colours of his Western travels. This set of 41 water-colours is now owned by the Public Archives of Canada.

Michael Bell is the director of the Agnes Etherington Art Centre, Queen's University, Kingston.

BRAVES AND BUFFALO

Plains Indian Life in 1837

Water-colours of Alfred J. Miller
with descriptive notes by the artist

Introduced by Michael Bell

The Public Archives of Canada Series
University of Toronto Press

© Information Canada 1973
ISBN 0-8020-2093-3
LC 73-85088
Printed in Canada

The Public Archives of Canada Series

General Editor: Hugh A. Taylor

Braves and Buffalo

Plains Indian Life in 1837

The water-colours illustrating this book were painted by Alfred Jacob Miller, a Baltimore artist who travelled to the Rocky Mountains in the early years of the nineteenth century. Miller's journey, a ruggedly adventurous undertaking for the time, was with a group of Eastern fur traders who were making their annual trek to Oregon where trappers congregated en masse in what was known as a 'rendezvous,' an event that combined selling the winter's take of pelts with the renewal of friendships, drunken brawls, and as much wenching as time and the availability of female companions would permit.

Miller accompanied an eccentric and romantic Scot, Captain William Drummond Stewart, a restless adventurer who had been on four previous rendezvous caravans. By 1837 the fur trade had already entered a decline. Stewart was in fact witnessing the beginning of the end of a significant way of life in the American West. It may have been a premonition of this which motivated him to commission Miller to record with his pencil and brush the thirteenth rendezvous of 1837.

Furs were the wealth of the northern reaches of the North American continent. In 1837 when Miller, Stewart, and their companions journeyed to the fur trappers' rendezvous, the Oregon Territory was still jointly occupied by the United States and Great Britain. Miller and Stewart joined the caravan of the American Fur Company, a firm owned by John Jacob Astor. The company's pack horses were laden with goods – rifles, traps, clothing, axes, hatchets, non-perishable foods – to trade off for the furs taken by the mountain men. (To the north, in what would become Canada, was the most active of the fur-trade giants, the Hudson's Bay Company, but it launched no such excursions. The HBC operated from fixed posts – often forts – to which the trappers, mainly Indians, brought their furs. Our only visual record of those posts at their peak comes from another frontier artist, Peter Rindisbacher, a Swiss-born painter who had emigrated to Canada in 1821.)

The rendezvous caravans carried with them the forces which would eventually undermine the fur trade. Missionaries travelled west with the caravans as did medical doctors, real estate speculators, and others with visions of quick wealth. All these men found their way to the Oregon Territory with the help of fur traders, and settled there. They carried with them the seeds of destruction of the very business which transported them.

In 1837, when Miller and Stewart joined Astor's caravan, Stewart took with him an entourage of about ten persons including the painter. The caravan set out from near Independence, Missouri, under the leadership of Tom Fitzpatrick, a tough veteran of the mountain trade. Stewart, who had served in the British cavalry in the wars against Napoleon, was a trained disciplinarian and, with four previous caravans behind him, was a respected member of the mountain men's close fraternity. As a result, he was given some duties as a deputy to Fitzpatrick.

Miller had to pull his own weight on the trip: he was granted no leniency by his tough-minded patron. Miller lived up to what was expected of him and in the process absorbed the yarns and the myths of the mountain trade. Over the nightly campfires he heard the whole saga, and enthusiastically experienced much of it himself: the Indians – Blackfeet, Pawnees, Oglala Sioux and the Snakes – never to be trusted because you could never tell when they had a 'bad heart' for you; the buffalo still ranging in vast herds over the prairies; the excitement of the buffalo hunt as the Indian guides ran them down to be killed for food; and, of course, the colourful, unfettered trappers themselves. All this Miller took in and recorded in his sketch book.

After five weeks of travelling the caravan reached Fort Laramie, the famous first wooden fort. Miller's painting is perhaps the only visual record of it extant. From Laramie the caravan crossed the River Platte in bull boats, moved on to the Sweetwater River and Independence Rock, passed Devil's Gate and Cut Rock. The caravan made its way along a winding route towards the eastern entrance of South Pass. Once through the pass, it proceeded to the rendezvous site at Green River, between the New Fork and Horse Creeks in the heart of the Rocky Mountains.

The object of all this overland toil, the rendezvous, was in the simplest terms a business operation: the season's furs from the mountains were exchanged for the supplies transported west by the caravans. The goods would support the trappers for a year until the next rendezvous.

For the mountain men the rendezvous was something more than business, pure and simple. It was, as Miller suggests, also a saturnalia. Raw alcohol mixed with honey flowed freely; it was a powerful drink with enough knockout power to make even the toughened mountain men wary. To the missionaries who came seeking new and agreeable tribes to convert, the extensive gambling and trade in Indian women was disgustingly sinful. Drunken Indians and trappers alike ran wild through the camp; fights broke out frequently and, fueled by the alcohol-honey cocktail, the occasional fight ended in death. Huge feasts of fat buffalo cow washed down with the ever-flowing alcohol, the exuberant joy of the mountain men at seeing old friends after a year's absence, and the colourful dances of the Snake Indians, all provided a spectacle that was soon to disappear.

For Stewart, one of the highlights of the rendezvous was the chance to return to his favourite camping and hunting grounds on the headwaters of New Fork Creek. This, his fifth rendezvous, was a chance for him to entertain some of his friends of the mountain brigades with the finer things of life. Cheeses, wines, brandy, and porter, carried across half a continent, were removed from Stewart's packs as he entertained his old comrades. On this trip he had even brought a suit of armour as a gift for a friend among the mountain men.

Stewart's pleasures were in hunting, fishing, and conversation with his rough-and-ready friends; Miller revelled in the colourful pageantry of the rendezvous.

Alfred Jacob Miller was but twenty-seven years old when Stewart hired him to record the caravan of 1837, so it is not surprising that he had little reputation yet as a painter. Born the son of a grocer in Baltimore on 2 January 1810, he had studied in the United States for a time with Thomas Sully, and showed enough youthful promise as a portraitist to attract the attention of Robert Gilmor, one of America's first art collectors and patrons. According to the fashion of the day, Miller was then sent off to Europe in 1833 to study at the École des Beaux Arts in Paris. It was the era of unabashed Romanticism and Miller followed established tradition by copying the old masters in the Louvre. He moved on to Rome and copied the Italian masters; he visited Horatio Greenough in Florence while the American sculptor was working on his famous George Washington figure. Then he moved on to Bologna, Venice, and possibly Switzerland before returning to Baltimore in 1834. But success did not visit his new studio. Miller moved on again, to what seemed to be – and indeed proved to be – more fertile ground, New Orleans. It was here that Stewart noticed his work and commissioned him to record the caravan and trappers' rendezvous.

In the fall of 1837 Miller returned from the rendezvous to New Orleans and began work on the paintings for his patron. In July 1838 paintings of his Western travels were exhibited in his native Baltimore; in 1839 the oil paintings commissioned by Stewart were exhibited in New York's Apollo Gallery before shipment to Stewart's home in Scotland, Murthly Castle.

In 1840 Miller journeyed to Scotland at Stewart's invitation to paint a further series of oils for his patron. By this time Stewart had succeeded his elder brother to the baronetcy of Grandtully. Perhaps the decor of a Scottish castle called for more subdued paintings than Miller's brilliant water-colours; at any rate the oils that Sir William commissioned to decorate his country home, and to remind him of his free and happy years in the West, are dark and murky. Stewart returned to North America for one last time in 1842. He died in Scotland in April 1871.

Miller passed the winter of 1841-2 in London, where he met George Catlin, another artist whose name came to be closely associated with the West. Then, flushed with success, he returned in 1842 to Baltimore and commenced a career as a successful although provincial portrait painter.

On public demand, Miller continued to produce copies of his original Western sketches. An examination of his account book reveals a continuous demand for Western subjects. Between 1858 and 1860 William T. Walters ordered two hundred Western water-colours which now form part of the collection of the Walters Art Gallery in Baltimore. Also in 1858, a certain William C. Wait ordered a series of thirty-seven, but this collection has not been located. A further series of forty subjects was commissioned by Alexander Brown of Liverpool: it is this series, now in the Public Archives of Canada, which illustrates this book. The collection was presented to the Archives in 1946 by descendants of Alexander Brown.

The later paintings, and indeed all the pictures produced from the original on-the-spot sketches, are studio pictures. They are characterized by a sense of completeness, careful draughtsmanship, high colouration, and a Rousseauism which increases as the Western experience moves farther into the artist's memory; the 'savage' Indian becomes nobler and nobler in Miller's work as the nineteenth century advances. Except for this lapse Miller remained faithful to his original sketches for the most part. To assist his memory, Miller kept written notes to accompany his sketches and these notes, as he revised them, form part of the 1867 commission.

These same notes – Miller's own words – accompany each water-colour illustrating this volume. Some of the views he expressed could not be countenanced today, for they are based on ignorance; but they do reflect the attitudes that prevailed in Miller's time and may cause us to think more about the values we have inherited and the extent to which we have changed them. The real importance of Miller's notes lies in the details of Plains life with which he supplemented his vivid paintings, and which are reproduced verbatim on the following pages.

Miller died in Baltimore in 1874, a success in his own time. He was respected in Maryland for his portraiture and known outside the state only for his Western paintings. His reputation languished for nearly three-quarters of a century. The great post-Depression surge of interest in Americana brought him back to his rightful place in the history of American art as the first artist to paint the Rocky Mountains.

Miller takes his place in the ranks of illustrators of the North American West alongside George Catlin, whose first Western trip (which stopped short of the Rockies) predated Miller's by five years, and Karl Bodmer, artist to the royal naturalist, Maximilian, Prince of Wied-Neuwied, who went west in 1833. But Catlin, although he was the most famous, was not the first painter in the North American West – which at this time was subject to no national boundaries and was as much north of the 49th parallel as it was south. Peter Rindisbacher painted the West in the early 1820s, after leaving Switzerland with his parents to settle in Lord Selkirk's Red River Colony. The historical record he made complements that of Miller.

What follows was the West of Alfred Miller. His water-colours and his notes speak for themselves. The record he left shows an integral part of the North American past – a way of life based on the buffalo and the horse which prevailed throughout the grasslands on both sides of the 49th parallel, and a fur-trading system which was to fall victim to the spread of settlement of which it was the unwitting carrier.

MICHAEL BELL

Water-colours of Alfred J. Miller

with descriptive notes by the artist

14   **Hunting the Buffalo. Attack with lances**

After coursing and wounding the Buffalo, the Indian Hunters have here got the animal at bay, on his knees, from loss of blood, but by no means conquered; he is now simply dangerous, and may start up on a sudden, when the word must be '*Sauve qui peut.*' The bay horse to the left is a trained animal, and his rider plants him near enough to give the *coup de grace* with his lance; he is aiming for a spot behind the fore-shoulder, where a blow will be fatal. The white horse is untrained, restive, and in revolt from fright and the smell of carnage, placing his rider *hors de combat*. Hunters in the distance are pursuing the retreating herd.

To the savage, every part of this noble animal is useful. To say nothing of the exquisite 'hump rib' and other choice bits, the hide he converts into an extempore boat to float his plunder, or a robe to protect him in winter, to cover his lodge or make him a bed; the horns, cleansed, serve him for drinking cups or receptacles for powder; the scalp, with its long bushy hair and horns attached, is indispensable when he joins the buffalo dance; with the sinews he covers his elk-horn bow, to give it strength and elasticity; he also manufactures from it the strongest thread possible for sewing his war dresses; and, lastly, he tips the arrows with the bones, fashions them into fishing hooks, etc.

The Hunters, when approaching these animals by stealth, wear a peculiar kind of cap, which has ears and a flap reaching to the shoulders. Under this guise, the Hunter is mistaken for a wolf, and is suffered to advance quite near. The mass of hair covering the forehead of the Buffalo obscures his sight, aiding the Trapper in his ruse.

In the sketch, three Bulls are lying down near the swell of a rolling prairie; a Trapper, in company with an Indian, is stealthily creeping along the rise; as the arrows of the Indian make no noise, he is privileged to shoot first, or indeed *ad libitum*, the Trapper reserving his fire until the animals regain their feet, when he instantly 'draws a bead,' using his ram-rod to steady his rifle.

This mode of hunting is only occasionally pursued, the attack with lances being the favourite method, because it affords more excitement, and gives the Buffalo, for whose pluck the Trappers have great admiration, a fairer chance.

These rifts are large chasms in certain districts of the prairie, formed by natural causes, and enlarged by heavy rains surging through them. When the Indians find a large herd of Buffalos in the vicinity of these precipices, a hasty council is called, and measures adopted for the wholesale destruction of these valuable animals. They instantly detach men on fleet horses, to proceed to the opposite side of the herd from the rift, with instructions to close in at a given signal; in a short time the whole body, perhaps 10,000 (literally blackening the prairie), are seen moving in the direction of the chasm. Indians appear in the midst of the herd goading them on with every species of weapon, when the whole mass of animals become panic stricken and rush on to inevitable destruction. The poor creatures cannot stop for a moment from the pressure of the crowd, until the brink is reached, when they topple over, falling headlong one upon another, forming, under a cloud of dust, vast hecatombs of victims. This terrible scene is not to be paralleled any where else in the world.

Sometimes it happens that the Indians get entangled and are hurled down with the Buffalo; almost a just retribution for the deplorable waste of animal life.

The subject of the sketch had a great reputation among his people for war-like qualities, and impressed us favourably with his manner and behaviour. In shewing him, amongst other novelties, the percussion lock, a new invention at that time, he expressed no surprise (a fact which is characteristic of the Indian race), but great curiosity and a strong desire to possess the new improvement; and made us understand that he was sensible of its advantages.

When he came to give a 'sitting' for a portrait, he was highly displeased and incensed to find that we were engaged in sketching another Indian, who had, according to our conception, a remarkably fine head. His reason for annoyance was that 'The Indian we were engaged upon was neither a *Brave*, *Warrior*, nor *Chief*; could count no *coups* nor shew any scalps in his lodge.' After this *exposé* we hurried through with the unfortunate subject, and *he* was glad to give place to the proud, supercilious, and arbitrary old Warrior who had denounced him in so summary a manner.

The eyes of 'High-lance' had the peculiar sleepy expression of a Lion in repose; but let the war-whoop be raised, and they would be lighted up instantly with devilish rage and passion; and the civil, well-mannered Indian be changed into a demon of the worst order. In fact, it may be said that they are all sleeping volcanoes subject to sudden outbursts of ungovernable fury.

The toilet of our sitter was quite complete. He had on a necklace of 'wampum,' which is rare, and difficult to be obtained; and the inevitable charm, or medicine, was suspended on his breast.

The Indian being a great observer of rank and position, it naturally follows that he is punctilious as regards etiquette; the sketch represents him riding out with his Squaw; her place being fifty yards or more in the rear of her liege-lord. She knows better than to ride near, or at the side of the 'great creature' in front. He is her master, and she worships him accordingly.

Although he is abominably tyrannical and arbitrary, yet it must be confessed that he dresses the lady and her horse in barbaric splendour; she is mounted '*a la Turque*,' with stirrups made of wood, and covered with bull's-hide. The saddle is adapted expressly for her convenience and safety; pounds of beads, and any number of hawks' bells are lavished on her dress and on the horse's trappings; at her side, depending from the saddle, hangs her 'possible sack,' which is a wonder of workmanship, in dyed porcupine quills, and in it she carries her trinkets and finery.

It would not do to examine her 'hero' too critically. We should probably find him proud, insolent, and overbearing; his thoughts and aspirations being, not how he should benefit his neighbour, but how he could contrive to do him the greatest amount of injury. His education having been neglected, he does not readily distinguish between '*meum*' and '*tuum*'; but he steals with a good conscience, really knowing no better, and following implicitly the example of his father before him.

34   Wild horses. Throwing the lasso

On the first intimation that a drove of these beautiful animals is in sight, preparations are made for their capture. The Indians provide themselves with Lassos of firmly twisted bull-hide, one end of which is secured to their horses, or to their persons, the slack of the rope is coiled in their hands, and the other end is made into a running noose.

As they approach the drove, the scene becomes intensely exciting; the Indians now riding in a perfectly reckless manner, their figures swaying to and fro with the motion of their steeds, display a rude natural grace.

On reaching the herd, each one selects his victim. They throw the Lasso at him with unerring dexterity, catching the animal by the neck or leg, as the opportunity presents itself. The horses are trained by long practice to brace themselves backward, as soon as the rope is thrown, in order to resist the strain.

38 Shoshonie woman throwing the lasso

As a general thing, women who are expert in throwing the Lasso, secure the horses in the evening who have strayed off when feeding, and some are so wild that it is impossible to catch them without resorting to the rope.

Occasionally, however, a woman takes the field (as in the present case) against wild animals. She is seated on a high demi-pique saddle, the pommel of which rises eighteen inches, the cantle twelve, and her feet rest in broad wooden stirrups. Mounted in this way she cannot well be unhorsed; while her long experience in catching tame horses is now brought into requisition. Her greatest danger is, after throwing the rope, to meet the strain, and this difficulty is met by giving her a well-trained horse.

There is another mode of catching the wild horse, which is called 'creasing.' The Hunter selects his animal from the herd, and fires at him, wounding him at the junction of the mane with the neck, stunning him so completely as to prostrate him. The Hunter then dismounts, rushes up and secures his feet with a Lasso, before he recovers from the temporary trance.

It will at once be apparent that this requires a good shot. If the aim is a little too high the ball is thrown away, if too low it kills the horse.

The principal lodge, that nearest in the sketch, is the council chamber; its diameter is about seventy feet; the light is admitted only from the top, through an aperture six feet in diameter; and this opening also gives egress to the smoke from a fire in the centre of the lodge.

The effect of light coming from above, and passing down through the column of smoke, is extremely curious and picturesque to an artist's eye.

The framing of the building is composed of poles, radiating from the centre, which are supported by uprights and girders, and roughly planked; the whole exterior is then covered with 'adobe.' From exposure to the sun this coating becomes very hard, firmly retaining its place, and being entirely water-proof.

On fine days, the Indians are fond of seating themselves on the roofs of these structures, making arrows, bows, and other implements, smoking and chatting.

The 'medicine man' also stands here in seasons of excessive drought 'to make it rain,' invoking the 'Great Spirit' to aid him.

Guards, too, from these points, watch the loose horses feeding on the prairie, and keep a vigilant eye on the horizon, to discover the first sign of an enemy.

The Warrior is waiting impatiently for his costume, for he always does his enemy the honour of making his best toilet before starting out to encounter him.

The dress is being made by his Squaw, it is sewn throughout with sinew, and is such a substantial and serviceable work, that it is often handed down to a second generation.

The body is formed of very soft tanned antelope skin, and tinted of a delicate salmon colour; the middle of the sleeves, shoulders, and front are profusely and brilliantly decorated with dyed porcupine quills of all colours, and with these are interwoven a variety of beads, locks from scalps, etc.

The cap or helmet, made of red cloth, is trimmed with eagle feathers. The war necklace, composed of bears' claws, is an evidence of his prowess over these formidable brutes, and great importance is attached to it. The bow, arrows and shield, are made by himself at leisure moments.

Hanging to the branch of a tree, is the papoose; when the mother is busy, the young one, in this manner, is placed out of harm's way. The probation of childhood is so severe that only strong and healthy children survive the exposure incidental to it.

The Dacotahs or Sioux, and Snake Indians, were the finest of the tribes of savages that we met in the north-west.

The sketch is from the head of a Sioux; selected more for the purpose of what we conceived to be a favourable specimen, than for any special celebrity either as chief or great warrior. His behaviour was that of a well-bred man, quiet and unobtrusive, his figure and bearing having a strong resemblance to a graceful antique statue in bronze. On his head he wore a tuft of richly dyed feathers attached to the scalp-lock. This latter appendage we were informed was not only for ornament, but religiously preserved for his enemy as a trophy in case of his defeat in battle; a long cue depended from it, reaching to his knees; ornamented at intervals with brass rings, the size of a doubloon at the neck and gradually lessening in size towards the end.

The Sioux are exceedingly warlike, and are almost always engaged in forays on their neighbours; they possess very fine lodges and war dresses, and an abundance of good horses.

The hunters are here taking a flying shot at a herd of Elk as they pass, for running the Elk is useless, their speed far outstripping that of the horse. The stratagems resorted to, are – creeping to the point of bluff when they are known to be lying under it; heading them off when practicable; forcing them into a river; or lying concealed at some point where they are likely to pass. When the Buffalo became scarce, we found the Elk to be a most desirable acquisition to the prairie larder, more from the quantity of meat than excellence as food, as we considered it inferior to either Buffalo, Bear, Mountain Sheep, or Antelope.

The Indians make a beautiful buckskin from the hides of the Elk, which is very soft, thick, and strong, and with which they make leggings, giving them a rich tint by a peculiar process of smoking. They also make the skin into sacks to carry their pemmican and jerked meat; and from the horns their most efficient bows are made.

The largest herds encountered by us did not exceed 300, but, as a general rule, there were not so many together, and they were very shy and wild.

Although an Indian's life is nearly worthless to any one but himself, yet he uses every means to preserve it, and often is indebted to his litheness, native cunning, and activity for its preservation. The 'duel' would not suit him at all, as he does not believe in fair play. In battle, if on foot, he chooses his ground, so that he may retreat behind bushes, trees, rocks, etc., in cases of emergency.

In skirmishing with his enemy on horseback, he makes a target of his horse; watching the arrow of his adversary with the eye of a hawk, when the occasion requires it, he, quick as lightning, clings to the horse's neck, dropping his body on the furthest side from his adversary. In this position he exposes but a part of his arm and leg, and sometimes he holds on simply by the heel, while the horse is in full motion.

In such an attitude he will discharge arrows under his horse's neck, recovering his seat in a moment if he wishes it. Of course this feat can only be attained by long practice, and a broken neck is sometimes the result of the first attempt.

This name was a misnomer, as the subject of it stood nearly six feet in his mocassins.

It did not apply in any way, for he was then Chief of about 3,000 Snake Indians, and decidedly superior to every one that we met.

He was a man of high principle, in whom you could place confidence. When our Commander, on a former journey, had a difficulty with the Indians, and lost all his horses, Ma-wo-ma exerted himself in his behalf, and recovered the most of them.

In making a drawing for me, such as they send as a sort of letter to their friends, he coloured the drawing with a stick; all four legs of the horse were drawn on the same side. His war horse, himself, and his immense helmet of eagle feathers, occupy the whole field, while the enemy are diminutive creatures, and whom he is spitting like larks. Fifteen arrows above the enemy signified that number had 'gone under,' but Ma-wo-ma, like a prudent general, says nothing of his own losses. A fac-simile of the letter is subjoined.

Fac-Simile of a drawing
made by Ma-wo-ma— Chief of Snake
Indians,— West of Rocky Mts.

The scene represented in the sketch is a Crow Indian riding to the point of a bluff to examine the prairie, and he forms an extremely picturesque subject, full of wild grace and beauty.

From these elevations their eyes sweep the horizon, and from long practice they discern an object much sooner than an inexperienced person could do; they observe in which direction game is to be had, the approach of an enemy, or of a caravan of 'pale faces,' and make their preparations accordingly.

At all times they are ready to give battle to the different tribes of Indians, but they generally try to conciliate the whites, experience having taught them that they usually come off second best in such encounters; besides, they always receive presents when they exhibit a friendly disposition, and as they appreciate kindness, the inexpensive favours they receive produce the best results.

As a general thing the reputation of the Crows was at a low ebb among the whites in Oregon, on account of their propensity to steal; and whenever they were in our vicinity, a double guard was mounted to protect our horses and property from their piracies.

72 **War ground. 'Beating a retreat'**

Although the Sioux Indians have an immense range of their own to hunt over, they are not content with it, and they often trespass on the grounds of the Blackfeet. The latter, from a bluff, have discovered the marauders, and are discharging their arrows at them, and are in a rage because they are not near enough to secure their scalps. The Indian in advance is defending himself as best he can. His shield is covered with bull's hide, and becomes so tough, in course of time, that no arrows can penetrate its surface. His greatest care is to protect his head and body, letting his arms and legs take their chance. In case an arrow penetrates one of them, he still continues his flight to a place of safety; and his capability of bearing pain, and patience under its infliction, are wonderful. When he is no longer pursued he sits down and cuts out the arrow, compressing the wound with a bandage drawn tightly round it, enclosing medicinal plants if they are to be found.

These circles are found on the upper waters of the Platte River. Buffalo skulls in great numbers, are placed in a ring twenty feet in diameter, the nasal bone of each pointing directly to the centre. The Trappers told us that they had found them in other districts made of human skulls, and supposed that they were connected with some superstitious rites. 'Medicine,' with the Indians, signifies charm or mystery.

They invoke two spirits, the good and the bad; but the latter being the most potent, is the most feared, and is to be conciliated at all hazards.

When Indians are seized with disease, the 'medicine-man,' is sent for; he visits his patient dressed and painted in savage magnificence; he usually commences with a most unearthly howl, sometimes rattling pebbles in a small drum, these, with other antics, are intended to exorcise the evil spirit.

They have, however, for fever, a better cure. A pit is dug, stones, heated very hot, are thrown into it; the patient, supported on a frame-work, is laid over the opening, and water poured on the hot stones. A buffalo robe encloses the steam generated around the patient.

In the right-hand corner of the sketch Hunters are departing for the chase. In the opposite corner, another party, with a sumpter mule well laden with meat, has just come in, and is waiting to report its proceedings; in a large body of men this becomes a matter of great importance.

A Caravan always comprises a heterogeneous mass of people from all parts of America, and of every variety of complexion. There are the Company's and the Free Trappers of the West, Half-breeds, French Canadians, Spaniards, Indians, etc., and, although we lost some of these by casualties, not a day's sickness occurred to any one during the whole journey, as far as we knew.

The government of the band was necessarily rather despotic, as our leader, who had served in the Peninsula under Wellington, well understood the management of reckless and unruly spirits. It was amusing to see how he checked bullying propensities. At the commencement of our journey, two of the men began fighting; when it was reported to him, his answer was 'let them alone;' at last one of them was so badly beaten that he could not 'come to time.' On learning this, our Commander sent for him, and he came before him in a sorry plight. 'Eh bien, Louis, you have been fighting, and look as if you had been well thrashed.' 'Oui, mon Capitain.' 'By jove, I am glad to hear it,' quoth the Captain; 'no doubt you richly deserved it, I shall have no further trouble with you, and am certain that *you* will not boast of it. You can go.' He now sent for the conqueror, who approached his presence with a jaunty and impudent air; whereupon the Captain (instead of complimenting him, as he fully expected) told him that if he ever heard of his bragging of having whipped Louis, he would dismount him and make him walk for a week.

This was cold comfort for the conqueror. The idea of winning the battle and not being suffered to boast, swept away all the glory of the thing; but the mode of treatment was effectual, and there was no more fighting among the men.

Men caught sleeping when placed on guard, are also deprived of their horses, and made to walk.

Antoine (a Half-breed) and three Indians are here congregated around a Buffalo they have killed. They have placed him in an upright posture, preparatory to securing the hump, side ribs, and choice bits. Wolves, watching them from a distance, impatiently await their share of the entertainment. When that incomparable piece, the hump rib, is brought into camp, Jean, our *Chef*, at once takes charge of it, and the manner in which he prepares it for the table, although simple enough, is perfection. He skewers it lengthwise, with a stick sharpened at one end, leaving sufficient room at the other end to plant it in the ground near the fire, inclining inward at the top. When done, it exceeds in flavour, richness, and juiciness, any beef we have ever tasted, and this judgment will be confirmed by all who have ever partaken of the glorious 'hump rib.'

Antoine (the half Indian) was our best hunter, and was appointed by our Commander to aid us in getting sketches of the Buffalo; this he did effectually, but in his own peculiar fashion, that is, he would have as much fun as possible. The animal, when wounded in the flank, would usually stand still for a time, and we would then ride near and take a sketch. Sometimes, while absorbed in drawing, the brute would suddenly make a dash at us, and a ludicrous scene would immediately ensue, convulsing our *fidus Achates* with boisterous merriment. As he was with us almost every day in these excursions, there was no lack of incidents and *contretemps* in which the ridiculous predominated. Antoine killed for the camp (single-handed) about 120 Buffalo in our outward journey; and although ordinarily good tempered, he was uncontrollable and dangerous when his Indian blood was roused.

88   A young Indian mother fording a stream

In the foreground of the sketch a young Indian mother with a papoose is crossing a stream. A band, secured to the board which supports the child, forming a sort of cradle, passes around her forehead, while her arms encircling the child secure it in a steady position. These cradles are of the most simple construction, but could not be safer or more efficient with any amount of elaboration. Two flaps of buckskin are fastened, one to each side of a board; the child is placed between them, and they are laced over it. A strong guard protects the head, and it may be thrown down with violence without the slightest injury to the occupant. In camp, it is usually hung on the limb of a tree or a lodge pole, where it may be rocked by the wind, while the mother attends to her domestic duties. Being bound to these boards when young, no doubt contributes, in a marked degree, to that straight, erect posture and carriage we notice in this people; indeed, we do not recollect, in the whole journey, seeing an Indian with a stoop in his shoulders (we encountered them often enough in civilized life). When it is time to release the children from this thraldom, they are tied on horseback in the midst of the packs, and soon learn to ride. On one occasion we saw a horse run away with a child of about three years old. The mother at once galloped after the little fellow, whose head seemed likely to roll off from the violence of the motion, yet the child instinctively tugged at the reins, when a Trapper overhauled him and stopped the horse.

These Indians are (comparatively) peaceful, and have other qualities that are rare and commendable. They are said to be honest and truthful in their intercourse with the Whites, and their observance of religious ceremonies and rites is uniform and remarkable.

It is supposed that they derived this, in great part, from the Catholic Missionaries who have travelled amongst them. Their ceremonial, however, is a mixture of the civilized and the barbarous, and, although they will not hunt on a *fête* day for fear of the Great Spirit, even if they are pinched with hunger, yet they are most inveterate gamblers, playing until all their possessions have been lost.

All these Indians seem to bear the impress of a doomed race, and they with bitterness of heart may exclaim:

'They waste us, aye, like April snow,
In the warm noon we shrink away;
And fast they follow as we go
Towards the setting day,
Till they shall fill the land, and we
Are driven into the Western sea.'

The ears of our subject are peculiarly ornamented, the rims are cut all round with a knife, and brought down with little weights; when these heal, many rings, sustaining strings of 'wampum,' are suspended to them. This he conceived to be very ornamental, and it is merely an exaggeration of a civilized lady's earrings, which is a relic of barbarism.

The Hunters are here in pursuit of the most formidable and ferocious animal to be met with on the journey. It is very dangerous sport, from the fact that he is often prompted to attack, instead of avoiding, the Hunters, and his armour of thick hide and hair is almost impenetrable to the bullet. But these circumstances only enhance the charm of the hunt to the reckless Trapper and wild Indian. To capture the grizzly Bear is considered a signal honour, and a great *coup*. The relating of it is the *crême de la crême* of stories at the campfire, listened to with the most eager attention, and admitting a vast amount of embellishment.

The account given of this Bear's winter retreat was interesting. His hiding-place was not under the ground, but under a snow-bank, with a deep bed of leaves to repose upon. He closed up the aperture by which he entered, leaving only a small hole for breathing through; there he lay torpid through the long winter, of course without food or any nourishment, except that which he obtained from licking his paws. A most curious thing is, that these Bears are said to come out in the spring, in good condition, losing flesh afterwards by running about.

They vary in colour from a dusky grey to a dark brown, always more or less grizzled, and weigh, often, from 1,800 to 2,000 pounds.

The sketch is derived from a simple incident that arrested the artist's eye. An Indian girl springing up to a branch of a tree, sustaining herself by the arms, and thereby forming an impromptu swing. In the genial season of youth, all around her exhilarated, amused, and invited her to be happy. Every object was tinted with prismatic colours, and shone with a celestial radiance –

> 'The common earth, the air, the skies,
> To her were opening Paradise.'

Her companion, seated at a little distance, watches with mute regard and animated expression her lithe and graceful motion; her elfin locks of long black hair are streaming in the wind, like the mane of a wild colt; to crown all, her picturesque, but scanty robe

> 'That floats as wild as mountain breezes,
>   Leaving every beauty free,
> To sink, or swell, as Heaven pleases.'

The sketch represents the interior of an Indian Lodge; here they hold their grand councils, and decide questions of war against neighbouring tribes.

> 'It was a lodge of ample size,
> But strange of structure and device;
> Of such materials as around
> The workman's hand had readiest found,
> While moss and clay and leaves combined
> To fence each crevice from the wind.'

In the centre, a number of Indians are seated round the fire, engaged in playing the 'game of hand.' In this play, the object hidden is a small piece of wood, called the *'caché,'* that may be readily concealed in the hand; this is passed through the hands of the party, while one of the number guesses where it is. A choral chant (accompanied by the beating of an Indian drum) is raised, and the excitement is increased by betting. The chant becomes faster and more furious as the bets are doubled and trebled, and does not cease until some one of the party has lost everything. Gambling is an all-absorbing passion with them, and it becomes a species of mental frenzy. Standing at a little distance, without knowing what was going on, their wild gesticulations and furious singing would convey the idea that they were a set of maniacs.

The sketch represents 'our mess' at the morning meal and Francois pouring out the coffee. The dishes on the table, or rather on the india-rubber cloth, were of the best block-tin, and the etiquette was quite rigid in some particulars; for instance, nothing like a fork, or substitute for it must be used, without you wished to raise a storm of ridicule about your ears. With the 'bowie knife,' you separated a rib from the mass in the centre of the table, seizing with your hand the lower end, and cutting away *à la discretion*. We had no bread during the whole journey. The attitude at meals was generally cross-legged, *à la mode Oriental*. Indians were meanwhile patiently standing near, in order to be ready for the 'second table,' eating enough at once to suffice them for three days.

On one occasion, our Commander, who had purchased some boxes of sardines at St. Louis (intending to keep them in reserve for sickness or other emergency) ordered one of them to be placed on the 'table.' It was a double box, and contained about a pint. A Trapper opened it, pronounced the contents fish, and emptied the whole on his plate. Seeing this, the Captain ordered out the whole lot of sardines, as he saw that nothing short of it would go round. He would not for the world have hinted to them that it was customary to eat only two or three as a relish. This breakfast must have cost him upwards of sixty dollars, but it furnished him a capital after-dinner story for Europe, and he considered *that* worth all the money.

The Indian Hunters have been lying in ambush, waiting for a herd of Elk, and, as they rush by, a volley is fired at them. They are so huddled together, and move so swiftly, that direct aim cannot be well taken. The great desideratum is to shoot quickly as they are interlaced, and an arrow is sure to strike some one of them and bring him down. The wariness and speed of these animals, together with their pluck and savageness when brought to bay, demand skilful and experienced hunters, endowed with courage, activity, and endurance.

The Elk, or, as they are sometimes called, the 'Wapiti,' are found, like the Buffalo, on the great plains of the West, which they seem to prefer to timbered country. If taken young, they are easily domesticated, and would make magnificent animals for a park; we saw two that had been trained to harness, and they were perfectly under the control of the driver.

The Indians make their choicest and most handsome bows of their large horns, although they are so crooked. We brought down some specimens whose antlers measured over four feet in length.

This post, built by Mr. Sublette, of St. Louis, is now owned by the American Fur Company. It is situated near the Nebraska River, in the vicinity of the Black Hills, and is of quadrangular form, with block houses at diagonal corners, to sweep the fronts in case of attack.

Over the main entrance is also a block house, in which is placed a cannon. Inside of the Fort there is a spacious area, surrounded by small cabins built of large logs. The roofs of these cabins reach within three feet of the tops of the palisades, against which they abut. The Indians encamp in great numbers around here several times in the year, bringing skins to be exchanged for dry goods, hardware, tobacco, and other articles.

They have a great dread of the 'big gun' which is mounted in the block house, having had experience of its prowess, and witnessed the havoc produced by its 'loud talk.' They are under the impression that it is only asleep, and have a salutary dread of its being waked up.

Mons. Fontenel was Commandant at the time of our visit. It was very strange to find in the reception room of the Fort four of five large engravings, for it reminded us of the far distant civilization of the 'States.'

At four o'clock in the morning, it is the duty of the last men on guard to loosen the horses from their pickets, in order to let them feed. At daylight everybody is up, and our cooks are busy with preparations for breakfast. Tents and lodges are thrown down, wrapped up, and bundled into the waggons. If the sun is twenty minutes above the horizon when breakfast is finished, we conceive he has a reproachful look. By this time the horses are driven in, and each man hurries after his own, to saddle or harness him, and the train proceeds *en route*.

A strong contrast is visible between the white and red man. While all is activity and bustle with the descendant of the Anglo-Saxon to get off in good time, as if he feared the Rocky Mountains would not wait for him, the Indian lingers to the last moment around the camp fire; he neither enters into, nor sympathises with, the diligence of the former, and seems to regret that stern necessity forces him to proceed.

The loiterers at the camp-fire on the prairie never fail to hear narratives of startling adventures, and of the hair-breadth escapes of the Trappers and Hunters, in their encounters with these *'mauvais sujets.'* They are the sworn enemies of *all*, Indians and White men alike. Their principal grievance against the latter is, that they trespass on their Beaver streams. Although they have been warned off repeatedly, and have been threatened with the consequences, the reckless Beaver Trappers pay not the slightest heed, and they are knocked on the head at the average of fifty per season.

The Blackfeet have undoubtedly the reputation of being the most warlike and aggressive of all the Indians of the North-West. Their very name is a terror to most of the other tribes, and they are so strong in numbers, and so determined in their vengeance, that indiscriminate slaughter follows every victory. But it is said that they do not fail to observe the rites of hospitality when they have no suspicion of treachery.

The sketch represents a party of Blackfeet on the war-trail; they are decidedly rough riders, and have very little mercy for their horses. It is an unlucky day for the party who meets these *'bête noirs.'*

In the sketch the plain is literally covered with these animals; they are to be counted by thousands, and are to be seen as far as the eye will reach. The Hunters are on the alert, and must have their wits about them, as it is no child's play. They dash without hesitation into the very midst of the moving mass of animals, being fearless, self-possessed and wide awake, and well mounted on trained horses, which are indispensable for their safety. Very little more can be seen of them than their heads and those of their horses. Their object is to select the best Buffalo or those which are (as they express it) 'seal fat.' Other Hunters have separated some more from the main herd, and are pursuing their game in all directions.

At the right of the sketch, a Buffalo, enraged beyond endurance by his persecutors, who have wounded him, is now charging them. Incited by pain, he means mischief, and bellows for revenge; understanding this perfectly, the wily Hunters 'vamose' for a time, but soon return to renew the battle with him, and wound him in a more vital part. At length, exhausted from loss of blood, he succumbs and rolls over in the dust.

The scene is in the vicinity of the Black Hills, and is highly characteristic of that district of country, being alternate plain, bluff, and mountain.

The Indians in selecting a Buffalo from the herd, when hunting, are much more influenced by the capability of his skin to be made into a good robe than by the apparent tenderness of the meat for eating. A party here have killed an animal, and in their exultation are sounding a yell of triumph and of victory. One of them, to be more emphatic, or to give the key-note, stands on the animal. No description can give an idea of this wild, ear-piercing shriek; it is something quite unearthly.

After the hide is secured, on their return to the lodges it is handed to the women, who are expert in preparing Buffalo robes for the market.

The Indians sometimes select a few of the robes, and paint on them reminiscences of battle-scenes, in the most brilliant colours, thereby enhancing their value, and causing them to command a premium at the agency of the Fur Company.

As the Buffalo are rapidly passing away, it seems strange that more efforts are not made for their domestication. Our Commander captured seven Buffalo, which he presented to the Marquis of Breadalbane, at Taymouth, Scotland, where we saw them, inclosed in a large paddock. They had become thoroughly tame, and some young Buffalo were calved on the estate.

136   Pawnee Indians watching the caravan

Of all the Indian tribes, the Pawnees gave us the most trouble, and were to be most zealously guarded against. We knew that the Blackfeet were our deadliest enemies, but fore-warned was to be fore-armed. The Pawnees professed amity. In passing through their country it was most desirable, and indeed essential, to cultivate their goodwill, but they required continual watching.

Whether they were within the camp, or in its vicinity, it was requisite to put a double guard over the horses. When we were '*en route*,' we were continually under their surveillance. From the tops of the bluffs, behind rocks, and out of the long grass of the prairie, they watched us, and kept themselves informed of our movements, transmitting, no doubt, the information to their 'head quarters.'

With such insinuating and prying varlets, it was difficult to act prudently. When the day came for quitting their dominions, we were glad to bid them farewell, at once relieved of all anxiety for our horses.

At the first appearance on the horizon of this dangerous visitor, the whole camp is aroused. The fire travels with the speed of a race-horse – Buffalo, and all kinds of game fly before it – licking up everything it encounters, and spreading in every direction. A dense cloud of smoke overshadows it. It is sometimes the result of accident, more frequently the work of Indians, and occurs in the fall, when the grass, being very long and dry, burns like tinder. No time is to be lost if the camp is to be saved, the order being given to set fire to the grass in the camp. While one party is setting fire to the grass, another follows closely, threshing out the flames to prevent them gaining too much headway, soon forming a burnt space, to which the horses and mules are hurried and closely picketed. They behave as badly as possible on such occasions, and give rise, on the part of the Trappers, to all manner of wicked expletives in French and English. When they are all secure, the same process is used to save the waggons; finally, the grass on the side of the camp nearest the approaching fire is lighted, in order to meet it. The remedy is effectual, and attended with less danger than an attempt to retreat.

The mode represented in the sketch of replenishing the larder is often resorted to very successfully, and as we had about 150 men to feed, it behoved the Hunters to be careful and prudent. A party of hungry men do not readily listen to reason, or admit excuses from an unfortunate Hunter with a good grace.

The Hunters having descried the animals at a distance, decide whether it is best to run, or approach them quietly. If the latter mode is adopted, as in the present case, they at once ascertain the direction of the wind; if it should be from the Buffalo, nothing can be more favourable, if not, they make a circuit until the difficulty is surmounted. The reason of this proceeding is, that the animal's power of scent is most acute, giving him alarm at the distance of a mile or more, but his sight, from the great mass of hair covering his head, is often obstructed.

The Hunters, reaching their position, hide their horses in a ravine, or behind bushes, and commence approaching on hands and knees. As they carry double-barreled rifles, and, in their lingo, shoot 'plum centre,' a Buffalo or two is often secured.

On this eventful morning, we descried one of our Hunters returning to the camp at full gallop, which was unusual. On reaching us
he pronounced one word, 'Indians!' Another arrived who was more
explanatory; he cried out, 'Ingins is all about, and thar will be
some raising of ha'r as sure as shootin';' this produced a silence of
some moments, a general gravity of countenance, and all eyes
turned in one direction. We were not kept long in suspense, a cloud
of dust soon raised, and discovered a piratical horde of painted
wretches armed, yelling hideously, and riding round us in a
menacing manner. We now stopped and held a parley. Their argu-
ment was simple – 'they were on their own ground, and we were
intruders.' The great point, was to get the Chiefs to smoking as
quickly as possible, in order to gain time, and hold a council. At
length we formed a circle, and put the pipe in circulation, each of
them taking a few whiffs, the first with much ceremony, and
looking towards the sun (the Great Spirit).

Learning that presents (black mail) would be acceptable, we
arranged matters on that footing, giving them blankets, knives,
tobacco, ammunition, etc. We were glad on these terms to get rid
of our most unwelcome guests, the Trappers invoking *peculiar*
blessings on their heads.

The scene before us represents a camp that has been suddenly roused by the guard at night. The drowsy Trappers seize their guns. The Blackfeet are in every direction, uttering frightful yells. The horses and mules struck with terror, snap their lariats, or force their pickets, and then make off at a rapid pace into the darkness with the Indians after them. The poor Trappers, confounded by the suddenness of this onslaught, and the quickness of their enemies' retreat, have little chance to repel them, their lives being but a poor recompense for the deplorable loss of all the horses and mules.

These raids at night are the lot of nearly all parties who journey to the Rocky Mountains (the Pawnees, Crows, and Blackfeet being adepts at them). The consequences are very serious, our Commander, on one occasion, losing nearly all his horses. The attack is so sudden, and the confusion consequent on waking up from sound sleep so bewildering, that little can be done before irreparable mischief ensues.

The animal has been wounded in the flank, but not disabled, and full of rage and pain is making savage onslaughts on his enemies, who, on their part, are tantalizing him with feints, and retreating as he gives battle. The Hunters are remarkably expert in evading the attacks of the unwieldly brute, their horses being more active and quicker in turning, have greatly the advantage in a skirmish of this kind.

It is worth remarking how nature prompts the Buffalos to preserve their health and comfort by a substitute for currying. The herd selects a sandy district, and one of them lies down; he makes a pivot of the centre of his body, begins vigorously pushing backwards with his fore-feet, and by this means revolves in a circle; when tired, another takes his place. In a short time, a basin is formed of sand, fitting their shape precisely, and alternately each resort to it. These round basins, or 'wallows,' are found wherever the ground is suitable for their formation.

He must also have his water-bath, as the above is an earth-bath. When it is added that he affects a particular kind of grass, called Buffalo grass, and that man offends his delicate nostrils at the distance of a mile and upwards, it must be granted that he is quite luxurious in his habits.

On the appearance of a large herd of Buffalo in their vicinity, the Indians make extensive preparations to 'surround' it, in order to destroy as many as possible.

Every thing being in readiness, 'runners' are appointed, generally the young men, mounted on fleet and well-trained horses, who move cautiously towards the herd, traversing ravines or hollows where practicable, and always in a position to have the wind from the Buffalo. On reaching their appointed places, the signal is given to a party in ambush, when all rush forward *pell mell*, and ride round the herd, contracting the circle closer and closer. They then begin to discharge their arrows, which throws the animals into confusion, and a panic ensues. Each Hunter now selects the fattest animal near him, riding fearlessly into the crowd of animals, and sometimes drives an arrow completely through one of them. In a situation of this kind, the Hunter is often exposed to imminent danger, either from the fall of his horse in Buffalo wallows, or from the infuriated Buffalo, who often turns suddenly on his pursuer. The horses seem to enjoy the sport as much as the riders, being dexterous in avoiding an onslaught.

The activity, native grace, and self-possession of the Indians, the intelligence of their well-trained horses, and the thousands of Buffalo moving in every direction over the broad and vast prairies, form a most extraordinary and unparalleled scene.

We found the tribe of Kansas encamped upon the Caw River, having become, by frequent intercourse with the Whites, semi-civilized. Their hunting is restricted to the black bear, black tail and common deer, turkeys, prairie hens, etc., as the large game has been driven away; and they also fish in the rivers, which are, however, well-stocked. They are instructed by government agents in agriculture, and succeed in raising a little grain. As their help was needed to get our waggons and charettes across the river without loss of time, presents were offered to them, but not a solitary man would stir. No! they wrapped their blankets around them, and stood looking at us with the most provoking coolness and characteristic stoicism, like so many bronze statues.

Some of them wore on their breasts large heavy medals of silver suspended from their necks by chains of the same material, having on one side a *basso relievo* of their 'great father,' J. Quincy Adams.

168   **A young woman of the Flat-Head tribe**

At the Rendevous on Green River, west of the Rocky Mountains, a large body of Indians had congregated, and as there were a variety of tribes represented, it gave us a fine opportunity to select specimens of each. It was there we met our present subject, who was pointed out to us as one of the belles of the Rocky Mountains, and we found little difficulty in obtaining her assent to sit for a likeness.

172 The 'rendezvous,' near Green River, Oregon

This was our final destination. Here we rested over a month, under the shadow of the great spurs of the Wind River Mountains, encamping among 3,000 Snake and other Indians, composed of Bannacks, Crows, Sioux, Aripahos, Chinooks, Cheyennes, Nez-Perces, Shotochoes, etc., who had all assembled here for a special purpose, viz., to trade buffalo robes and skins, for blankets, guns, ammunition, tobacco, and a variety of smaller articles.

The first day is given up, by established custom, to a species of Saturnalia. Gambling, racing, boxing, and drinking are in the ascendant. On the second and succeeding days all this is changed. The American Fur Company's great tent is elevated, and trading goes briskly forward. Here the Trappers get their outfit, departing, under the command of a leader, for the beaver streams. Here we saw all the celebrities, both Indians and Pale-faces.

In the sketch, our Commander, after making valuable presents to his friends, is now smoking the 'pipe of peace' with them.

The Alfred Jacob Miller Collection

Hunting the Buffalo. Attack with Lances Signed *A.J. Miller* 8 x 13¹/₄
Approaching the Buffalo Signed with *A.J.M.* monogram 8³/₄ x 12
Buffalo Rift Signed *A.J. Miller* 8³/₄ x 13⁷/₈
Schim-a-co-che ('High Lance'). A Crow Indian Signed *A.J. Miller Pᵗ* 11⁷/₈ x 9³/₈
Indian Warrior and his Squaw Signed *A.J. Miller* 8⁷/₈ x 11³/₄
Wild Horses. Throwing the Lasso Signed *A.J. Miller* 8³/₄ x 11¹/₂
Shoshonie Woman. Throwing the Lasso Signed *A.J. Miller* 9¹/₈ x 11⁵/₈
Indian Village. On the Missouri Signed with *A.J.M.* monogram 8⁷/₈ x 14¹/₈
Indian Woman making the War Dress Signed with *A.J.M.* monogram 9⁷/₈ x 8¹/₄
Head of a Sioux Indian Signed with *A.J.M.* monogram 6⁷/₈ x 6
Shooting Elk Signed *A.J. Miller* 8³/₄ x 11⁷/₈
Skirmishing. Crow Indians Signed *A.J. Miller* 8³/₄ x 11³/₄
Ma-wo-ma. 'Little Chief' Signed *A.J. Miller Pᵗ* 11³/₄ x 9³/₄
Fac-Simile of a Drawing made by Ma-wo-ma — Chief of Snake Indians, — West of Rocky Mts 7³/₄ x 9³/₄
A Reconnoitre Signed *A.J. Miller* 11⁵/₈ x 9⁵/₈
War Ground. 'Beating a Retreat' Signed *A.J. Miller* 9¹/₂ x 14¹/₄
Medicine Circles Signed with *A.J.M.* monogram 8⁷/₈ x 12
Caravan 'En Route' Signed *A.J.Miller* 8⁵/₈ x 15⁵/₈
Camp Providers Signed *A.J. Miller Pᵗ* 7⁷/₈ x 11³/₄
A Young Indian Mother Fording a Stream Signed *A.J. Miller Pᵗ* 11⁷/₈ x 9⁵/₈
Nez-Perces Indian Signed *A.J. Miller Pᵗ* 12 x 9³/₈
The Grizzly Bear 8 x 12³/₈
Indian Girls Signed *A.J. Miller Pᵗ* 11⁵/₈ x 9¹/₄
Indian Lodge Signed *A.J. Miller Pᵗ* 7⁷/₈ x 12
Breakfast at Sunrise Signed *A.J. Miller Pt* 8³/₈ x 11³/₄
Herd of Elk Signed *A.J. Miller Pt* 8¹/₈ x 11³/₄
Fort Laramie Signed *A.J. Miller Pᵗ* 8⁷/₈ x 12¹/₂
Breaking up Camp at Sunrise Signed *A.J. Miller Pt* 7⁷/₈ x 14¹/₄
The Blackfeet Signed *A.J. Miller Pᵗ* 9⁷/₈ x 14³/₄
Hunting the Buffalo in Herds Signed *A.J. Miller Pᵗ* 9¹/₄ x 14⁷/₈
The Yell of Triumph Signed *A.J. Miller Pt* 8¹/₄ x 14³/₄
Pawnee Indians Watching the Caravan Signed *A.J. Miller Pᵗ* 11³/₄ x 9⁵/₈
Prairie on Fire Signed *A.J. Miller Pᵗ* 8¹/₂ x 14¹/₈
Approaching Buffalo Signed *A.J. Miller Pᵗ* 7³/₄ x 11⁵/₈
Pawnee Indians on the War-Path Signed *A.J. Miller Pᵗ* 8¹/₂ x 14
Stampede by Blackfeet Indians Signed *A.J. Miller Pt.* (?) 8⁵/₈ x 12¹/₂
Buffalo Hunt Signed *A.J. Miller Pt* 9 x 15³/₈
A 'Surround' Signed *A. J. Miller Pᵗ* 10¹/₈ x 17¹/₈
A Kansas Indian Signed *A. J. Miller Pᵗ* 11³/₄ x 9³/₈
A Young Woman of the Flat-Head Tribe Signed *A. J. Miller Pᵗ* 11³/₄ x 9¹/₂
The 'Rendezvous', near Green River, Oregon Signed *A.J. Miller Pt* 7⁵/₈ x 14¹/₈

The Public Archives of Canada collection of Alfred Jacob Miller water-colours was donated to the Archives by Mrs. J.B. Jardine, a descendant of Sir Alexander Hargreaves Brown, who commissioned the copies of the originals in 1867. Each water-colour was laid down and matted and titled by the artist. Measurements are to the nearest one-eighth of an inch, vertical x horizontal.